Mama's CHURCH Hattitude

Published by HenschelHAUS Publishing, Inc.
www.HenschelHAUSBooks.com
Milwaukee, Wisconsin

ISBN: f978159598-797-6

I want to dedicate this book to my mother, Zennie M. Burge, and all women who continue the legacy of wearing church hats. Special tributes to these women: Sis. Audrey Ramsey (the Queen of Hats), Sis. Luella Dallas (deceased), Mother Ruby Cockfield (deceased), and Mother Beatrice Carter (deceased). Mother Carter would always say, "When you go to church, you are not dressed without a hat on your head." Special thanks to my cousin Nathaniel for photographing the hats.

Contents

PART I

Introduction: Brief History about Church Hats

But every woman that prayeth or prophesieth with her head uncovered dishonoureth her head: for that is even all one as if she were shaven. (1 Corinthians 11:5)

The tradition for wearing church hats originated from the apostle Paul's words that women should cover their heads during worship service. For African American women, these words became an inspiration for a fashion movement that led to them covering their heads with elaborate church hats.

In the early twentieth century, most African American women were working six days a week in positions that required them to wear uniforms and aprons. Sunday was the day that the Lord said, "Remember the Sabbath and keep it holy." That meant they traded in their uniforms and aprons for church clothes and matching hats adorned with everything decorative, from bows, flowers, and ribbons. They finished their attires with matching gloves, high heels, and purses. And don't forget the silk stockings (most often your only selection was Red Foxx). Know that a woman wearing a beautiful church hat today is wearing history, a status symbol, not vain glory.

On August 28, 1963, Mahalia Jackson captured history when she sang "How I Got Over" at Dr. King's March on Washington, wearing a flowery hat. She sang "You know my soul looks back and wonder how I got over." Symbolic of struggles, her hat was her crown, representing all women.

Aretha Franklin wore a giant, stiff hat with a crystal-embellished bow to President Obama's inauguration on January 20, 2009.

When Duchess Kate Middleton wore her fascinator millinery-style hair piece, it not only turned heads but inspired more women to wear hats. Even Jennifer Hudson joined in on the hat parade at Aretha Franklin's funeral. The real show stopper was Cicely Tyson, whose face you could barely see hidden beneath a gigantic black head covering.

Church Hat Rules

- Never wear a hat that's wider than your shoulders.
- Don't wear a hat that's darker than your shoes.
- On Easter Sunday, wear a cream-colored or pastel hat, even if over six inches of snow is covering the grass.
- Never let the feathers on your hat get ruffled.

Church Hat Rituals

- Press hair, using a hot comb.
- Put on Fashion Fair makeup (a little red on the cheeks).
- Use Red Foxx stockings.
- Slip on pointed-toe shoes.
- Match your purse and gloves.
- Dress in a suit tailored to fit.
- Wear a hat (crown on head).

PART II

Narrative about Mama's Hats

Mom,

My inspiration for writing this book was an "aha" moment looking at all of your hats stacked in boxes that weren't labeled. I could only imagine what they looked like, and then I thought, *I'll just take them down and label each box.* But this project was put on hold, and I returned home to Wisconsin. Each time I see a beautiful church hat, I think about your hats. Even though you are in Mississippi, I can picture you sitting under your beautiful hats, praising God.

I was blessed to return to Mississippi for Mother's Day. My sister Pearl said, "You are just in time to be a part of our Mother's Day Hat Parade." I wasn't over-joyed, because I don't wear hats, but I went along with the idea.

That week before Mother's Day, I remember Pearl and I going on our hat adventure through your collection. Just as I remembered, the boxes were stacked up to the ceiling and were not labeled. Each box we opened held a special treasure—oohs and aahs! Some of them I recognized because I had purchased them. As we tried on the hats to make our selections, I felt like one of the stepsisters in Cinderella. Some of the hats were too big, and some were too small for my face.

Soon you became curious, stuck your head in the doorway, and started to laugh as you watched us place hats on our heads and pretend to walk like the church ladies. You joined in the adventure by sharing the story behind each hat. You explained, "The gold one with the wide brim is the one I wore to my sister's golden anniversary."

As you were sharing your story, my mind drifted back to when we were children. Pearl, Sadie, and I were all part of your hat stories. On Sunday mornings, you would get us all dressed up for church. Our Sunday dresses had petticoats that could be seen when we walked. Ribbons and bows were on each braid. You would inspect us to make sure we were church ready, that our legs were well greased—no ashy legs. We would then wait on the couch in the living room until you got dressed.

You would sit in front of the mirror and style your shoulder-length hair that had been pressed and curled. You would make sure every curl was in place. After applying your makeup, you would put on your jewelry. The finishing touch was your hat. As you placed it carefully on your head, you would tilt it slightly so that it covered one eye.

After that, you would turn your attention back to our last-minute instructions, making sure we had pocketbook money for Sunday School. You would then get your purse, Bible, and gloves. When you were ready to make your exit, under the admiring eye of Dad, you would glance in the mirror, over your shoulder, and in a whisper as you winked, say, "Girl, you know you are sitting under that hat!"

When we arrived at church, you would enter the sanctuary with your head held high. It was as if that hat had transformed you into the epitome of gracefulness. You moved with a **hat attitude** that made a statement of being a queen and your hat was your crown. Although the hat was tilted over your eye, the top pointed upward to heaven, catching God's eye.

I watched the other ladies of the church as they made their grand entrances. They would strut like colorful peacocks under the adornment of hats of all sizes, shapes, and colors. Some had Scripture overtures of "My Cup Runneth Over" and "Overflows with Joy." As I watched those ladies praising God, making a joyful noise to the Lord for all of His benefits, you would never know what they had gone through the past week.

My mind shifted back to the present as you continued to share your church story about hats. You said, "When I was growing up, all of the ladies I knew wore hats to church. The men would always remove their hats when the ladies walked past." You stated that hats were used to take up offerings in church. I thought to myself, *Maybe that's where the phrase "pass the hat" came from.*

Remembering your story about the Sunday when you and your best friend were returning home from church visiting, I could see that was book material. As I recall, you said she was driving with the window down when suddenly the wind blew her hat off.

You said, "It was the day of Pentecost. The hat took off on Holy Ghost wings and flew out the window." Your friend turned the steering wheel loose, reached over her shoulder, grabbed her hat, foot still on the accelerator, and the car ran off the road into the ditch and out again without stopping. You held onto your hat, thanking God as you thought of the words to the song, "I'm going to take a trip on that good old gospel ship, and we'll go sailing through the air." The hat went sailing through the air, it was retrieved, and the car never stopped until the two of you reached your house.

I asked if you were afraid, and you said, "I didn't have time to become afraid. I just held on to my hat—that's my crown."

Every one of your hats has its own story. As you sat beneath each one, it would receive a spiritual anointing, whether through song, prayer, meditation, or joyful thanksgiving. Here is a small sample of your beautiful hats.

PART III

Photos of Mama's Hats, What Some Meant When She Wore Them

My Steering Wheel Hat

When my friend let go of the steering wheel, sitting beneath this hat I could say, "Jesus, take the wheel. My friend just let go, but I know you are in control! Amen."

My Steering Wheel Hat

Psalm 46:10, Cease striving and know that I'm God

What is this life but filled with striving;
Fighting against others to take control of the driving.
My steering wheel of life, I firmly hold;
Trying to maintain my control.
Moving from one obstacle to the other, trying to find my
way;
Until the Spirit speaks to my heart saying,
"You need to Pray!"
Lord, I know that you know what lies ahead,
The path that you've already tread.
I release my control on the wheel
As you speak to my soul saying, "Peace be still"
(Matthew 8:23-27).

My I Love the Lord, He Heard My Cry Hat

This hat has been anointed with my tears of joy for the many times the Lord has heard my cry.

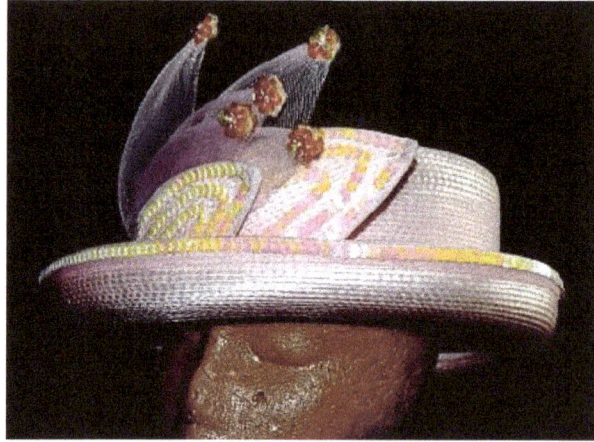

What A Friend We Have in Jesus

What a friend we have in Jesus.
Our sins on Calvary's cross He did bear.
When we get weary along life's journey,
kneel and pray to the one who does care.
He will give you peace that the world can't understand;
Our Savior that was sent to redeem the fallen man.
Run to Him when you are troubled and can't seem to find
your way;
He is always faithful when in his word we learn to obey.

My 23rd Psalm Hat

My favorite Scripture reminds me that no matter where my journey takes me, the Lord, my Shepherd, is my Constant Companion, Caretaker, Father, and Provider who refreshes my soul because He is always by my side.

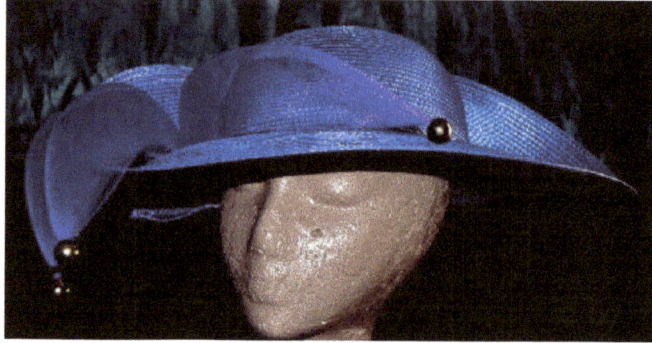

Styling

She put on her stockings; straightening the seam.
Her purse matches her shoes, you see, they are a team.
The feather on her hat matches her dress
Making the statement, "This is my Sunday Best."
Everything is matching from head to toe;
Even the pin on her shoulder has a shiny glow.
She enters into the sanctuary and takes her seat,
Moving to the rhythm of the choir, not missing a beat.
Her praises go to the Lord above
As she honors Him with reverence and love.
The hat on her head implies "This is my crown"
The message is clear "I'm heaven bound."

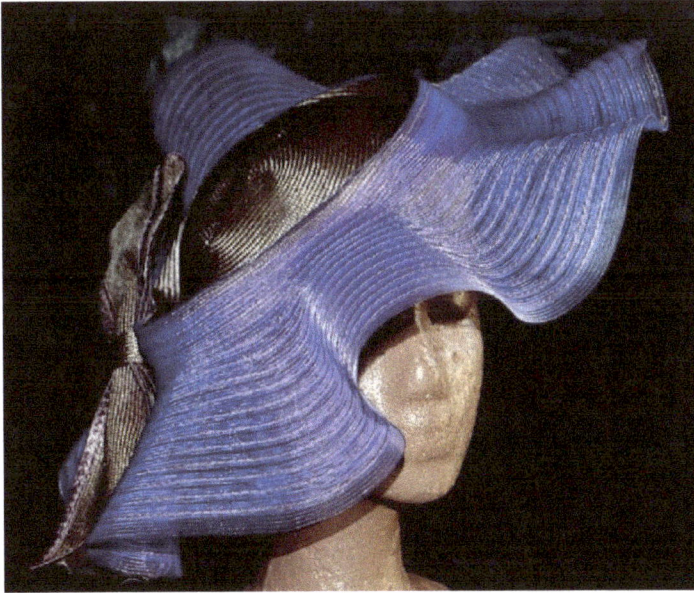

My Lord's Prayer Hat

Acknowledging that God is mighty, eternal, and powerful, my prayer beneath this hat is that I am to be used as a vessel for God's purpose and service.

My Prayer Hat

*When I go into my secret closet, I close the door as I pray,
in faith and confidence, knowing that God will answer
through His divine providence.*

*My hat of prayer has many colors like the awe-inspiring rainbow
that reminds me of my many seasons of life; a mixture of joys and
sorrows. When the storm clouds appear, I'm, sometimes, en-
gulfed by the darkness; but as the tumultuous thunder rolls, and
the lightning's flash across the sky, I'm, always, reminded that a
beautiful rainbow will eventually appear.*

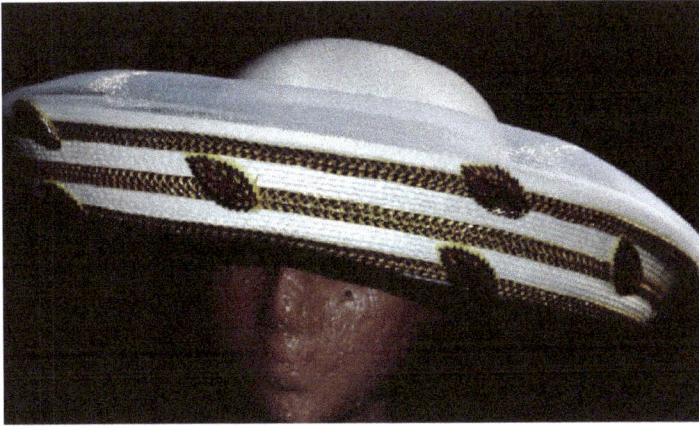

My *Amazing Grace* Hat

Sitting beneath this hat, I sing of how God's Amazing Grace has brought me through many dangers, seen and unseen.

Grace Hat

A woman's church hat is worn with dignity and grace,
Matching the perfection of the makeup on her face.
That woman of grace knows how to sit under a hat
As she sings along with the song "This, This and That."
Her flamboyant hat sways to the beat
As she keeps the rhythm with the tap of her feet.
Other ladies will look out of the corner of their eyes
At that beautiful hat pointing to the sky.
Her hat leans, slightly, to the side
As she sings long with the choir, "Jesus You are my
Guide."
She is wearing that hat with so much style;
I just say to myself, "Sister, you got it going on"
as I give her a smile.

My Convention Hat

Wearing my convention hat, I am increasing my knowledge of the Word of God to share with my church so we are reminded that we have an Anchor in our times of need as we try to help others with their spiritual growth.

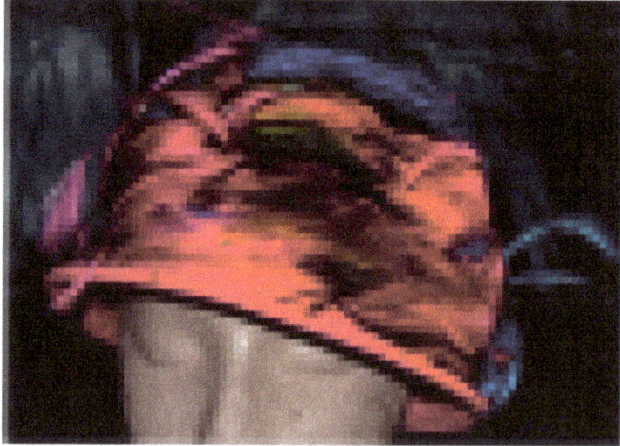

Now thanks be to God who always leads us in triumph in Christ, and through us diffuses the fragrance of His knowledge in every place. For we are to God the fragrance of Christ among those who are being saved and among those who are perishing.
2 Corinthians 2:14–15

My Sister Gave Me This Hat

Each time I sit beneath this hat, I think about my sister and thank God for her.

My Family Reunion Hat

When I get dressed for my family reunion, the last thing that I put on is my hat because it brings on thoughts of excitement, anticipation, and the feeling that I just can't wait to get there. When I finally arrive, I can hardly contain my eagerness to reconnect with each generation whether old, young or in-between. It's an opportunity to bridge the gaps and fill-in the missing pieces to our family stories that connect us; preserving our family legacy.

When I look at all of the families, I'm reminded of the Old Oak Tree in my yard. Like that Old Oak Tree, many have lost some of their bark, limbs and/or branches. Yet, like that Old Oak Tree, they have weathered the many storms and are still standing.

When I look at the branches that extend from the tree, it is a reminder that our lives within this family may extend in many directions still our roots remain the same. We continue our family legacy by building unity and creating traditions. Our family is founded on faith, united in love and kept by God.

When the reunion is over, we hug and say goodbye. As we leave, we pick up our treasure box of made memories and tuck them away within our hearts. Before another year some may be called home, waiting for us in heaven for the grandest family reunion of all where we will never have to say goodbye again.

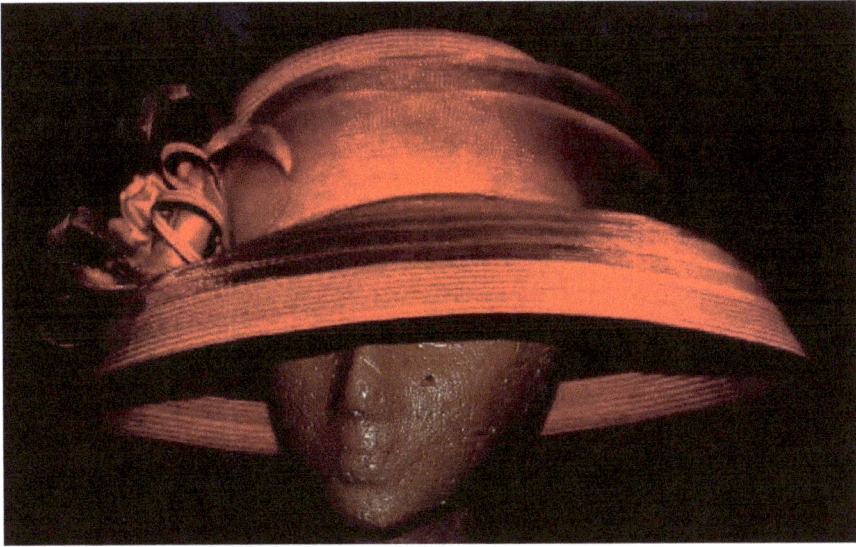

My It's a Blessing Hats

When I'm asked to sing this song, the Holy Spirit takes over and I become a vessel being used by God.

Hat of Compassion

I wear my hat of compassion;
It never goes out of fashion.
Therefore, I must wear it for all seasons;
In the Bible you will find the reasons.
Seeing the needs of others with our heart,
That's why we must start
With compassion and empathy;
We must look at one another through love and humanity.
From Jesus, we must take heed
And show compassion to others in need.
As we travel our own Emmaus Road,
Find a way to lift someone's load.
Rather than ponder why are you there?
Reach out your hand for his burden to share.
Walk in faith with a good Samaritan's stride;
Don't pass him by and go to the other side.

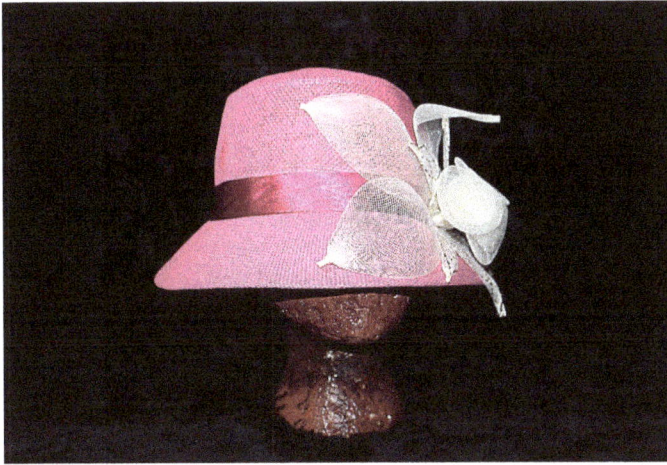

My Doctor's Visit Hat

I wear my little turban hat on my doctor visits. It's my telling-the-doctor-all-about-my-aches-and-pains hat. I remind the doctor that I might be old, but I can still communicate with him.

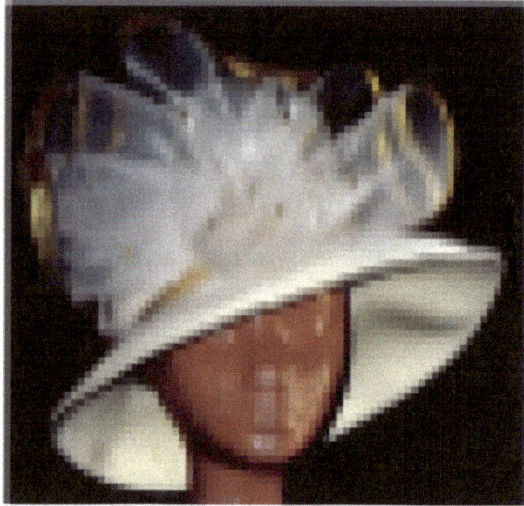

Lord, according to Your Word, my body is a temple. I must take care of it daily. That requires proper nutrition, exercise, and medical care. Most importantly, spiritual housecleaning.

My Blueberry Picking Straw Hat

This hat shields me from the sun and allows me to pick the best blueberries.

My Blueberry Picking Hat

Getting up early in the morning to pick fresh blueberries is exhilarating, and refreshing as dew lingering on each berry; a reminder of blessings from God. Zechariah 8:12 talks about the vine giving her fruit, the earth giving produce, and the heavens giving dew. My early time picking blueberries becomes my cherished time with God. I'm reminded how Jesus got up early in the morning, and went to a secluded place for prayer. Watching the sunrise, I lift my eyes toward heaven, with praise and thanksgiving, I honor God with the fruits of my lips; thanking Him for saving my soul, and giving me a loving family and friends; looking forward to sharing my fresh blueberry pie with them as I share with them the health benefits of blueberries:

- Antioxidant rich
- Help prevent cancer
- Improve blood pressure
- Protect your heart
- Eating a cup of blueberries per day reduces cardiovascular disease

Isn't that just like Jesus, creating something that is not only delicious, but good for your health!

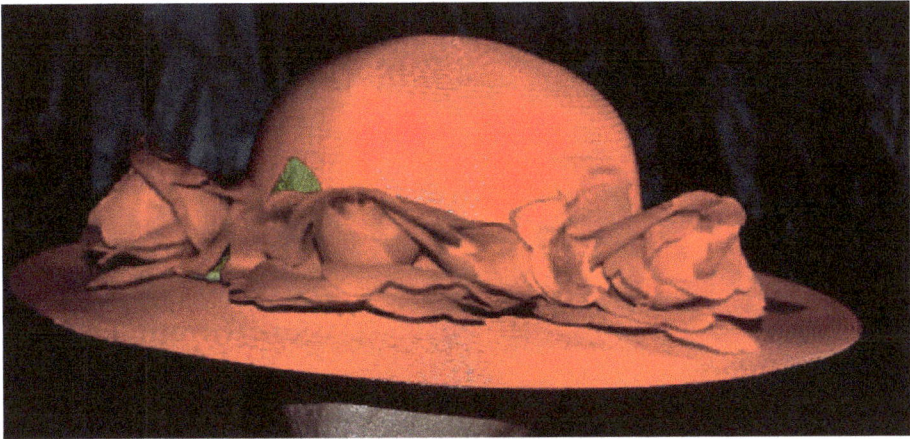

Consider the lilies, how they grow: they neither toil nor spin; and yet I say to you, even Solomon in all his glory was not arrayed like one of these. If then God so clothes the grass, which today is in the field and tomorrow is thrown into the oven, how much more will He clothe you, O you of little faith?
Luke 12:27–28

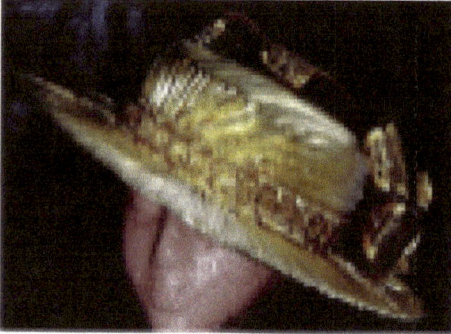

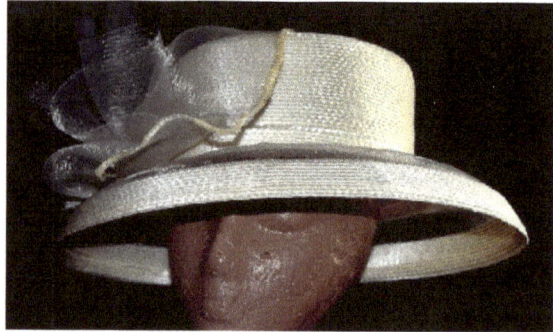

My All My Children Hats

On different occasions, like Mother's Day, my children shower me with hats that come in many styles, shapes, and colors. Sitting under these hats, I reflect on God's favor in my life through my children.

PART IV

Legacy Page: The Reader Can Write Their Own Narrative about Their Loved Ones' Church Hats

When your loved ones are gone, what do you do with their hats? Everyone's sentiments will be different. The mother of a friend of mine had an array of exquisite and flamboyant hats. When her mother passed away, my friend gave those hats to the ladies in her church. She stated that "As she worships on Sundays, looking around the sanctuary she can see Madea's hats and knows she is still worshiping in spirit."

What Are the Memories of Your Loved Ones'
(mom, sister, aunt, cousin, etc.) Church Hats?

Photo of Favorite Hat:

Most Memorable Occasion for Wearing This Hat:

Who Will I Pass This Hat Narrative on To?

www.ingramcontent.com/pod-product-compliance
Lightning Source LLC
Chambersburg PA
CBHW061407090426
42739CB00020B/3495